Tall Tales

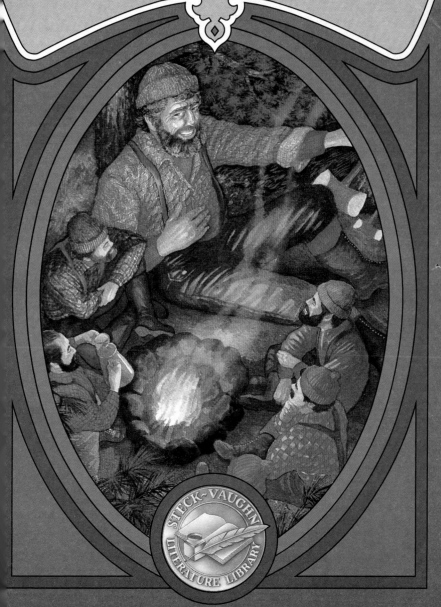

STECK-VAUGHN LITERATURE LIBRARY

*This book is dedicated to all folk tale collectors
and storytellers of the past, present, and future,
without whom these stories would be lost.*

Project Editor: Anne Rose Souby
Cover Designer: D. Childress

Product Development and Design: Kirchoff/Wohlberg, Inc.

Editorial Director: Mary Jane Martin
Managing Editor: Nancy Pernick
Project Director: Alice Boynton
Graphic Designer: Richarda Hellner

The credits and acknowledgments that appear on page 80
are hereby made a part of this copyright page.

Library of Congress Cataloging-in-Publication Data
Tall tales.
p.   cm.—(Folk tales from around the world)
Summary: A collection of eight tall tales featuring
such legendary heroes as Finn McCoul, Paul Bunyan,
Pecos Bill, Sally Ann Crockett, and John Darling.
ISBN 0-8114-2406-5 (lib. bdg.)
ISBN 0-8114-4156-3 (pbk.)
1. Tales. 2. Tall tales. [1. Folklore. 2. Tall tales.] I. Steck-Vaughn Company.
II. Series: Folk tales from around the world (Austin, Tex.)
PZ8.1.T15   1990
398.22—dc20   89-11504   CIP   AC

Printed in the United States of America.

1 2 3 4 5 6 7 8 9 0   UN   93 92 91 90 89

Steck-Vaughn Literature Library
Folk Tales From Around the World

ANIMAL TALES
HUMOROUS TALES
TALL TALES
TALES OF THE WISE AND FOOLISH
TALES OF WONDER
TALES OF TRICKERY
TALES OF THE HEART
TALES OF JUSTICE
TALES OF NATURE
TALES OF CHALLENGE

Program Consultants

Frances Bennie, Ed.D.
Principal
Wescove School
West Covina, California

Barbara Coulter, Ed.D.
Director
Department of Communication Arts
Detroit Public Schools
Detroit, Michigan

Renee Levitt
Educational Consultant
Scarsdale, New York

Louise Matteoni, Ph.D.
Professor of Education
Brooklyn College
City University of New York
New York, New York

CONTENTS

Oonagh and the Giants

by Toni McCarty

Who invented the tall tale? We Americans like to believe we did. But stories that stretch the imagination are as old as the hills. These stories are found throughout our land and in countries all over the world.

This tall tale from Ireland takes place in a land of giants. But the heroine, Oonagh, is not a giant. Even though she does not stand out for her size, she does stand out for her brain power.

ONAGH'S husband was a giant, a famous Irish giant, Finn McCoul. Big and strong as he was, there was another even tougher than Finn: Cucullin. Yes, Cucullin was truly a *giant* of a giant, and even Finn was scared of him.

Finn was afraid with good reason, for when Cucullin stamped his foot, the ground shook for miles around. He was tall as a church tower. Once he had punched a bolt of lightning down from the sky and pounded it flat as a pancake with his fist. He still carried that bolt of lightning in his pocket, flashing it with great pride whenever he felt like boasting.

One day Cucullin decided to fight with Finn. Finn heard he was coming and moaned. "What hope is there for me? Cucullin'll flatten me for sure if he catches me. And if I run, the green hills will laugh at me forever. Woe is me, poor Finn!"

"Now, hold on, husband," said his wife. "Leave it to Oonagh. Old Cucullin will never lay a finger on you."

"Don't even *speak* of his finger," Finn cried. "All of his strength lies in the middle finger of his right hand."

"And a nice fact that is to know," Oonagh answered. She reached in her work basket and picked out nine long strands of wool yarn, each a different color. She made three braids. One braid she tied around her right arm, the second around her right ankle, and the third and longest she tied over her heart.

When Finn saw this, he felt a bit of hope. Oonagh knew her share of the fairy wisdom and had her special way of doing things. This wouldn't be the first time she'd set things right.

"I'll be off to the neighbors," Oonagh said to her husband. "You just sit tight." She kissed him and left.

When she returned, she had all the iron griddles she could lay her hands on. She set to work making a pile of dough, then rolled it into flat, round cakes. Inside each cake, she hid a griddle. Only one cake did she bake in the proper way, with no pan inside it, and she set that cake apart from the rest.

"Now, Finn, put on this bonnet. Ah, it only sits on the top of your head, but it does look sweet, now, don't it! And wrap this lace around you like a baby's little gown—that's it—and climb into the cradle, dear."

Finn just stood there. "Our children are all grown up now, Oonagh. Must I play at being my own baby?"

But Oonagh was busy boiling up a sackful of cabbage and a side of bacon. "No time to argue," she called to him. Finn climbed into the cradle and kept quiet.

Suddenly there was a pounding on the door that shook the house. "Is that Finn McCoul there?" roared Cucullin.

Oonagh opened the door. "Finn's out and about, but come on in, mighty man."

Cucullin was twice as big as Finn, so he had to duck his head to get through the doorway. "I've come to fight Finn, I'll be telling you the truth."

"Well, sit yourself down if you wish. He's out looking for you, if Cucullin you be. What a terrible temper my Finn is in. I'm afraid he'll make a mess of you, poor wretched soul. A powerful giant is Finn McCoul!"

"Ha!" Cucullin laughed. "We'll see about that."

Oonagh began to cough. "Oh, dear. The smoke's coming down the chimney again. If Finn were home, he'd just turn the house around so's the wind couldn't blow down the chimney like that. But I don't suppose you could do it. . . ."

"Of course I can!" said Cucullin. Back outside he went, Oonagh following behind. She watched the giant pull on the middle finger of his right hand and heard it give three little cracks. Then Cucullin put his huge arms around the stone house, and puffing heavily, he turned it around.

In the house, Finn's cradle rocked wildly, and he shuddered.

"Now that you've been so kind," said Oonagh, "I'd like to fix your last meal for you. It'll take awhile, I'm sorry to say, for I need to fetch water down the hill. Ah, yes, today Finn was going to tear open our mountain, out behind the house, so we'd not have so far to go for water. But then, 'tis a job only Finn himself could do. Don't be troubling yourself with thinking you should try."

"Try?" bellowed Cucullin. "Anything Cucullin tries he can do!" said the giant. But he was beginning to wonder about this Finn. Tearing apart a mountain made of solid rock was no small feat, even for Cucullin.

Once, twice, three times Cucullin pulled on his

middle finger, cracking it nine times in all. Then he dug his big hands into the rock and pulled with all his might until—*Crack! Crumble!*—the mountain split wide open for a quarter of a mile, and the water ran free. The crack is still there; these days they call it Lumford's Glen.

When Cucullin came back in the house, he was beginning to worry about meeting up with Finn. These chores that Finn did around the house were almost too much for Cucullin himself.

"Now, sit yourself down and eat up," said Oonagh, dishing up a huge bowl of cabbage and piling up the griddle cakes in front of Cucullin.

The giant bit into one of the cakes and let out a yell. "What's wrong with this cake?"

"Why, that's just the way Finn loves them. But then, you take such dainty little bites. . . ."

At this, Cucullin opened his mouth wide and bit down on the cake as hard as he could. His giant tooth cracked. He let out a yowl so ferocious that Finn in his cradle howled in fear.

Oonagh said, "There, now. You've awakened the baby with your hollering. Well, one of my griddle cakes will make him feel better." She picked up the cake without an iron pan. "Eat it, little one," she said to Finn.

Cucullin could hardly believe his eyes when he

saw the size of the baby in the cradle. The baby gobbled the cake as if it were made of air.

"Is it special teeth this Finn family's got?" asked Cucullin.

"Come and see for yourself," said Oonagh. "They're way back in his mouth, so best you feel with your longest finger." Oonagh grabbed Cucullin's middle finger and stuck it deep into Finn's mouth. Chomp! Finn bit down with all his strength, and off came Cucullin's magic finger.

Now Finn felt brave as could be. Up he jumped and chased Cucullin out of the house and down the mountainside, roaring like a bull all the way.

Oonagh watched him proudly as he ran. "And doesn't he look sweet in that bonnet!" she said.

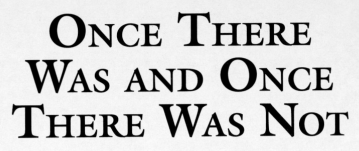

ONCE THERE WAS AND ONCE THERE WAS NOT

BY LEE WYNDHAM

Some of the funniest folk tales are stories that exaggerate the truth. And when tall tale tellers get together, the truth can really start to stretch. Any subject will do, as long as the lie is plenty B-I-G!

This tale about a proud storyteller is from Armenia, a part of southern Russia. Instead of starting the stories with "Once upon a time," the storyteller always begins, "Once there was and once there was not."

THERE was once a storyteller named Kasim, who lived in the busy oasis city of Tashkent. This city was in the southern part of Russia. Here travelers came and went to and from India, China, Turkey, Persia, and every other rich land of the Orient.

In the Tashkent camps of the traders, storytellers were always welcome, but Kasim was a great favorite. He could tell the most fantastic tall tales. Every one of his stories began with "Once there was and once there was not." And from the moment he said these words, everyone sat breathless, listening. After each tale, the traders showered Kasim with coins and praise.

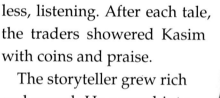

The storyteller grew rich and proud. He moved into a large house and dressed himself in splendid robes.

He put on the grandest airs, as if he were the chief *padishah*, ruler of the whole region. The traders put up with his silly manners for the sake of his stories, but they laughed at him behind his back.

One day, two of the younger travelers decided to teach Kasim a lesson. When he swaggered over to the camp fire, they seated themselves near him. Then, while Kasim told one of his tall tales, they raised their voices in an argument.

"I say Kasim has the greater skill as a story-teller," said one.

"Bah! He is as nothing to Ali-djan from my home village on the Aral Sea," the other declared.

"Hush! We cannot hear. Quiet, you!" From all sides, the traders ordered the two young men to be still.

But the name of Ali-djan stayed in Kasim's mind and buzzed there like an imprisoned fly. As the days passed, he seemed to hear the name of Ali-djan whispered wherever he went. *"Ali-djan! ALI-DJAN!"* The fly in Kasim's mind buzzed louder and louder until he could not bear it.

For his own peace of mind, and to prove once and for all that *he* was the more skillful teller of tall tales, Kasim decided to find this Ali-djan and challenge him to a contest.

No sooner thought than done. Kasim found out

the name of Ali-djan's village and set off at once. He journeyed by horse and camel across desert waste. He sailed by boat down the Syr Darya, which emptied into the inland Aral Sea. At the very edge of the sea was this village, and there was the house of Ali-djan.

Kasim looked at the tiny flat-roofed house and sniffed. Ali-djan could not be much of a story-teller and live in such a small humble house, he decided.

He puffed out his chest, strode to the door, and banged upon it. A small girl of six or seven, with eyes as black as ripe olives, opened the door.

"My father is not at home," she told Kasim.

Kasim was disappointed.

"When your father returns," he said to the little girl, "tell him that his fame as a storyteller has reached my ears. Tell him that I, Kasim of Tashkent, have come all this way to honor him. And I have brought him a gift of a Turkemen rug. The end of the rug I have left aboard the ship which brought me. The rest of the rug is at this moment being unrolled into your father's house by hired men. I wish him to see the whole rug and decide what use he can make of it in his home."

"Now," thought Kasim, "let us see how this Ali-djan will improve on my tall tale."

The little girl peered down the road toward the sea. She saw the ship at the dock. But there were no men unrolling a rug. Her eyes sparkled, and she clapped her hands, exclaiming, "Oh, how very lucky this is! You see, we have a Turkemen rug in our house. But yesterday a spark flew from the fire and burned a hole in it. Your Turkemen rug will be just right to make a patch over this little hole."

Kasim stared hard at the little girl. He could scarcely believe his ears. His eyes bulged, his breath grew short, and his face turned purple. He grasped his head between his hands and rocked from side to side. "Alack!" he cried, "if the small daughter of this Ali-djan can think up such a tall tale, how much greater must be the storytelling skill of her father!"

With that, he hurried back to the ship for the return journey to Tashkent. Kasim, the proud storyteller, was now a wiser and a humbler man.

THE TALL TALES

BY I. K. JUNNE

Stories about telling stories are found in many countries. In these tales, the main characters are the storytellers themselves. Often they try to outdo each other. Each story becomes more unbelievable than the one before.

This tall tale about telling tall tales comes from Burma, a country in Southeast Asia. It is about three brothers who dream up a lying contest. Will one of them win?

THERE once lived three brothers who were known throughout the land for the tall tales they told. They would travel from place to place telling their strange stories to those who would listen. No one ever believed their tales and all who heard them would cry out with exclamations of disbelief.

One day while traveling very far from home the three brothers came upon a wealthy prince. The prince was dressed very elegantly and bedecked in jewels such as the three men had never seen in their lives. They thought how wonderful it would be to have such possessions. So they devised a plan whereby they could use their storytelling ability to trick the prince out of his belongings.

They said to the prince, "Let's tell each other stories of past adventures. If anyone should doubt the truth of what the other is saying then that person must become a slave to the others." Now the brothers had no use for a slave. But if they could make the prince their slave then they could take his clothes because the clothes would then belong to them.

The prince agreed to their plan. The brothers were sure they would win because no one had ever heard their stories without uttering cries of disbelief. And so they found a passer-by and asked him to act as judge in the matter. All sat down under the shade of a tree and the storytelling began.

The first brother stood up to tell his tale. With a smile on his face he began to speak. "When I was a young boy I thought it would be fun to hide from my brothers. I climbed the tallest tree in our village and remained there all day while my brothers searched high and low for me. When night fell my brothers gave up the search and returned home. It was then that I realized that I was unable to climb down the tree. But I knew I could get down with the help of a rope. So I went to the nearest cottage and borrowed a rope and was then able to climb down the tree and return home."

When the prince heard this ridiculous story he did not make a comment but merely stood and waited for the next story to begin. The three brothers were quite surprised but were sure that the second story would not be believed by the prince. And so the second brother began his tale. "That day when my brother hid from us I was searching for him in the forest. I saw something run into the bushes. Thinking it was my brother I ran in after it. When I got into the bushes I saw that it was not my brother but a huge hungry tiger. He opened his mouth to devour me. I jumped inside and crawled into his belly before he could chew me up. When inside I started jumping up and down and making loud, fierce noises. The beast did not know what was happening. He became so frightened that he spit me out with such force that I traveled several hundred feet through the air and landed back in the middle of our village. And so though I was but a young lad I saved our whole village from the fearful tiger, because never again did the beast come near our village."

After this story the prince once again made no

comment. He merely asked that the third story begin. The three brothers were quite upset by this and as the last brother began his tale he had quite a frown upon his face. But he was still quite determined to make up a story so absurd that the prince could not this time help but doubt its truthfulness. And so he began his tale. "One day I was walking along the banks of the river. I saw that all the fishermen seemed quite unhappy. I inquired as to why they seemed so sad. They therefore informed me that they had not caught one fish in a week and their families were going hungry as a result. I told them that I would try and help them. So I dove into the water and was immediately transformed into a fish. I swam around until I saw the source of the problem. A giant fish had eaten all the smaller fish and was himself avoiding the fishermen's nets. When this giant saw me he came toward me and was about to devour me. But I changed back to human form and slashed the fish open with my sword. The fish inside his belly were then able to escape. Many swam right into the waiting nets. When I returned to shore many of the fish were so thankful that I had saved them that they returned with me. When the fishermen saw all these fish jumping onto shore after me they were indeed pleased and rewarded me."

When this story was finished the prince did not doubt a word of it. The three brothers were quite upset, but they knew that they would not doubt the words of the prince. And so the prince began his tale. "I am a prince of great wealth and property. I am on the road in search of three slaves who have escaped from me. I have searched high and low for them as they were very valuable property. I was about to give up the search when I met you three fellows. But now my search is ended because I have found my missing slaves. You gentlemen are they."

When the brothers heard these words they were shocked. If they agreed to the prince's story then they were admitting that they were his slaves. But if they doubted what he said then they lost the bet and became his slaves anyway. The brothers were so upset by the cleverness of the prince that they said not a word. The passer-by who was judging the contest declared that the prince had won the wager.

The prince did not make slaves of these men. Instead he allowed them to return to their village with the promise that they would never tell tall tales again. And the three brothers were thereafter known throughout the land for their honesty and truthfulness.

YOUNG PAUL BUNYAN

BY ROBERTA STRAUSS FEUERLICHT

American tall tales were born more than one hundred years ago and grew with America. The heroes and heroines in these stories are bigger than life. Just like the pioneers, they have a great spirit of adventure.

Paul Bunyan may well be our most famous tall tale character. He was larger than life from the day he was born. His childhood was as unusual as his size—at least, that's what this tall tale tells us.

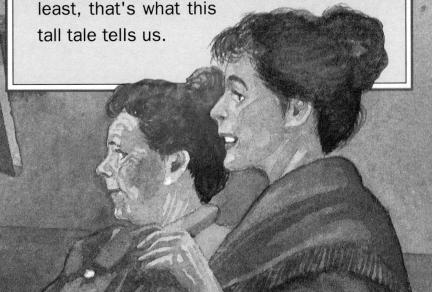

YOU would think that when a fellow like Paul Bunyan was born there would be such a holler the whole world would hear it and there would be no mistaking afterward just when and where it happened. But maybe everybody was so busy running around looking for a cradle big enough for the boy that they didn't have time to say anything, so now nobody is sure just where he arrived. Everybody is claiming Paul was born in one state or another or even in Canada.

The Canadians say Paul was born on Prince Edward Island, off the eastern coast. The first time he opened his little baby mouth and cried, all the lifeboats put out to sea. They thought the fishing boats were in distress.

An hour after Paul was born he weighed fifty pounds. He grew so rapidly that all the women on the island worked at their looms night and day but they couldn't weave fast enough to keep him in shirts. There were no buttons big enough for his first little suit, so they had to sew on the wheels of a wheelbarrow.

The only place big enough to christen Paul was the Gulf of St. Lawrence. Some volunteers were lowering him into the Gulf with a crane when the chain broke. Paul hit the water with such a splash there was a tidal wave in the Bay of Fundy.

At least that's what the French Canadians say.

Paul himself used to say he was born in Maine, which seems about right because logging was born in Maine too. And as everybody knows, Paul Bunyan invented logging.

From the beginning Paul was too big to sleep in the farmhouse up in Maine, so his folks put him to bed outdoors. But one night he got restless. He rolled over and flattened forty acres of timber.

The people in the village complained so much that Paul's father took all the timber that was already down and built Paul a cradle. He put the cradle, with Paul in it of course, out in the Atlantic Ocean, hoping the waves would rock the baby to sleep. But Paul rolled over in his cradle, as babies often do, and the waves he made swept away three villages along the coast.

Paul's folks saw that the cradle wasn't working too well, so they hollered to him to wake up and wade home. But Paul slept pretty soundly for a baby and he didn't hear them. They were afraid that if he rolled over again some more coastal villages would be swamped, so they called out the American navy. The whole fleet came and fired off all their guns, figuring the noise would wake Paul up, but the American navy was pretty small then and Paul didn't hear a thing.

So the American navy sent for the British navy and His Majesty's ships fired off volley after volley for seven hours before Paul heard the racket.

When he finally climbed out of his cradle and waded to shore, the waves sank every single one of the British men-of-war. Paul's folks felt pretty terrible about that. And so they gave the King of England the timber from Paul's cradle and with it he was able to build a whole new navy.

After what happened with the navy, Paul's folks built a special house made of rubber for him and kept him there until he was old enough to go to school. He was pretty good at helping his father out around the farm. He could kick out the potatoes so fast that his father grew three crops a year.

Paul's troubles started all over again when he got to the schoolhouse. When a fellow comes along who's different from the others somebody is sure to turn on him. This time it was the teacher. He just didn't know how to handle the boy.

Of course Paul's size was a problem. He needed four desks and his head stuck up the chimney. His books had to be hauled to school in a cart, and

then the teacher allowed him to bring only one a day because the schoolhouse wasn't big enough to hold any more.

Just to write his name Paul had to put five copy books one on top of the other, and even then the teacher would only see part of each letter, so he would mark him wrong.

The real trouble started over a pencil. The pencils the other boys used were so small they would get caught under Paul's fingernail. So he went out into the forest and pulled up a fir tree. Then he stripped off the branches and the roots and sharpened one end.

When he brought his pencil tree to school the next day the teacher got mad.

"Why can't you use a pencil like all the other boys?" he demanded.

"I'm not like the other boys," said Paul. To prove it he picked up the teacher, stuffed him into the stove, and went home. Luckily it was a warm day in late spring and the stove wasn't lit. But Paul's folks knew the boy could never return to school.

"What are you going to do now, Son?" asked his father.

"I don't know, Pa," he said. "I'd like to go to work but I can't think of a job big enough for me."

"You're right," said Mr. Bunyan. "There isn't a job in the world big enough for you right now. You'll have to invent one."

Paul went off for a walk to think about it a bit and the first thing he saw was the trees. You can't look in any direction in Maine without seeing the trees. And it came to him all at once.

"I'm big," he thought, "but so is America. I'm tall, but so are the trees. I'm strong, but so are other men. I'll make up a crew of the hardiest, bravest men I can find and we'll go out and chop down the trees so that they can be used to build America."

He went back and told his father, and Mr. Bunyan was pleased. "I haven't much to give you to start you off," he said, "but you're bound to need an ox to help you haul logs from the woods. A little ox was born today—the same day as the logging industry—and I want you to have him."

Mr. Bunyan took Paul into the barn and gave him a newborn white ox. Paul warmed it in his arms. "Because you are only a baby I will call you Babe," he said.

And with the little ox under his arm Paul waved good-by to his folks and set off into the woods to begin logging.

And that's how Paul used to tell of his birth and boyhood up in Maine.

There's still another story that claims Paul Bunyan was never a baby at all. He was born a full-grown logger with a black mustache and even white teeth and an ax in one hand and a crosscut saw in the other.

And that might be true, too. With a fellow like Paul Bunyan there's no way of knowing.

THE WINTER OF THE BLUE SNOW

BY DELL J. MCCORMICK

Paul Bunyan is one of America's very first superheroes. Stories about Paul came to life in the Northeast more than a century ago. Lumbermen would sit around the camp stoves during long winter nights. They loved telling tall tales about loggers much like themselves. With each telling, the stories became more and more fantastic. Have you heard the one about Paul Bunyan and the time it snowed blue snow?

ONE night in the North Woods the men were seated around a campfire. They were telling of their adventures in other camps. Someone asked Paul to tell them of his earlier adventures.

"Tell us about the Winter of the Blue Snow," cried Tiny Tim.

"Well," said Paul, "I was out logging with my father back in the Maine woods. That was the winter I found Babe the Blue Ox. Only he was a little calf then not much larger than Tiny Tim. Old-timers sometimes speak of it as the year of the two winters. When summer came, it got cold again, and in the fall it turned colder. For two solid years the snow covered the ground so deep that only the tops of the tallest trees showed through the snow.

"The snow was blue in color and over two hundred feet deep in places. The Great Lakes froze solid to the very bottom and would never have thawed out if loggers hadn't cut the ice up into small blocks and set them out in the sun to melt. When spring finally came, they had to get a complete new set of fish for the lakes.

"The camp was buried under the snow, and the men rode up to the surface in elevators. Each man had sixteen blankets so that he would be warm at night. Shot Gunderson, who was head sawyer,

can tell you how cold it was. He slept under forty-two blankets, and one morning he got lost and couldn't find his way out. It was three days before we could find him. By that time he had almost starved to death.

"It was so cold that when Hot Biscuit Slim set the coffee out to cool it froze so fast the ice was hot. The men had to eat breakfast with their mittens on. Sometimes the hot biscuits were frozen solid before they could take a bite.

"The bunkhouses where we slept were so cold that the words froze as soon as the men spoke. The frozen words were thrown in a pile behind the stove, and the men would have to wait until the words thawed out before they knew what was being said. When the men sang, the music froze and the following spring the woods were full of music as odd bits of song gradually thawed out.

"Very few trees were cut that winter as we had to make holes in the snow and lower the men down to the trees. Then we would pull the trees out of the holes with long ropes.

"The men all let their beards grow long as a protection against the cold. Some of the beards were so long that they got in the way, and the men were always stumbling over them. So we made a new rule in the camp. Anyone with a beard over six feet long had to keep the end of it tucked in his boots. In the spring the beards were so thick the men had to shave them off with axes.

"When Christmas came that year the men were homesick for some good old-fashioned white snow. 'It doesn't seem like Christmas,' they cried, 'with all this bright blue snow on the ground.'

"So I decided to put on snowshoes and travel west until I could find some white snow. Well, sir, I climbed over mountains and across plains right out to the Pacific Ocean, which was frozen solid. The ice seemed fairly thick, so I kept on going. And do you know I had to travel clear to China before I could find any white snow! But the men were certainly happy when I brought them back some white snow for Christmas!

"We had a lot of trouble with frost-biters that winter. They were little animals about three inches long that lived in the snow. They bit the men on the feet as they walked along. Even now, you hear of people being frostbitten, but that winter it was much more dangerous.

"The blue snow finally melted in the spring and filled many lakes in the woods. To this day, many of the beautiful lakes in the mountains are still colored blue from the Winter of the Blue Snow. The Indians called the country 'The Land of the Sky Blue Water.' "

PECOS BILL
BY LEIGH PECK

Just as loggers had their superhero in big Paul Bunyan, cowboys had their own superhero—Pecos Bill. Unlike Paul Bunyan, Pecos Bill didn't start out larger than life. But he grew into quite a legend. It is said that Bill invented the lasso and spurs. And he could even rope a tornado!

Cowhands told tall tales about this folk hero around their campfires. This story starts with Pecos Bill's strange childhood.

PECOS Bill lived in Texas when he was little. One day his mother heard that a new neighbor had moved in only fifty miles away. She decided, "This part of Texas is getting too crowded. We must move out where we will have more room."

So Pecos Bill's father hitched the old spotted cow and the old red mule to the covered wagon. The father and mother put their eighteen children into the wagon, and they started over the prairie. Their son Bill was four years old then. He sat in the very end of the wagon, with his feet hanging out.

When they were driving through the low waters of the Pecos River, one wheel of the wagon hit a rock, and the jolt threw Bill right out of the wagon and onto the sand of the river. No one saw him fall or heard him call, "Wait for me!" After Bill saw that the wagon was going on without him, he got up and ran after it. But his short little legs could not go so fast as the wagon. Soon it was gone, and Bill was left all alone. There were still seventeen children in the wagon, and no one noticed that little Bill was gone until his mother counted the children at dinnertime.

"Where is Bill?" she asked.

No one had seen him since they had crossed the

river. So the family hurried back to the river and hunted for little Bill. They looked and looked, but they could not find him. Because they had lost him at the Pecos River, they always spoke of him after that as their little lost Pecos Bill.

Little Pecos Bill was not lost for long. His father and mother never did find him, but he was found by an old grandfather coyote named Grampy. Grampy showed little Pecos Bill berries to eat, dug up roots for him, and found mesquite beans for him, too. At night Grampy led Pecos Bill to his cave in the mountain, where he could sleep safe and warm. Grampy showed his man-child to each of the other hunting animals and asked them not to hurt little Pecos Bill.

The bear grunted, "*W-f-f-f!* I will not hurt your man-child. I will show him where to find wild honey in the bee trees."

The wolf yelped, "I will not hurt your man-child. Let him come play with my cubs."

But the rattlesnake shook his rattles, "*Th-r-r-r!*" and hissed, "*S-s-s-s!* Keep him out of my way! I bite anybody that crosses my path, but I give fair warning first. *Th-r-r-r! S-s-s-s!*"

The mountain lion yowled, "Get your child out

of my way before I eat him up! A nice fat man-child is what I like to eat best of all!"

But all the other animals except the rattlesnake and the mountain lion promised to be good to little Pecos Bill. He learned to talk to all the animals and birds in their own languages.

But the coyotes liked Pecos Bill best of all. They taught him how to hunt. When he grew older, he was able to run so fast that he could catch the long-eared jackrabbit and the long-tailed road-runner. Finally he grew big enough to catch the deer, and even the antelope, which runs fastest of any animal. He grew strong enough to pull down a buffalo for his brother coyotes. He climbed the mountaintops and jumped about from crag to crag to catch the mountain sheep.

When one of the coyotes got a cactus thorn in his foot or a porcupine quill in his nose, Pecos Bill pulled it out. The coyotes were all very proud of their brother and very fond of him. At night he went out on the prairie with the coyotes and howled. He thought he was a coyote.

In all the years while Pecos Bill was living with the coyotes, he had never seen a human being. Then one day Bill's brother Chuck came riding along on his cow pony and found Bill. Bill was a tall young man now, his skin was a dark brown color, and his black hair hung long and tangled. But Chuck knew him at once, and cried, "Why, you are my long-lost brother, Pecos Bill!"

Bill replied, "I'm not your brother! I am the brother of the coyotes. Why, I even have fleas!"

But Chuck replied, "That doesn't prove you are a coyote. Why, all cowboys have a few fleas!"

"But I howl at the moon at night," Bill insisted, and he sang a little song:

> *"I'm wild and woolly and full of fleas,*
> *Never been curried below the knees,*
> *And this is my night to howl—*
> *Yippe-e-e-e!"*

Chuck repeated, "That doesn't prove a thing. All cowboys howl sometimes!" Then he added, "Look in the spring with me here, and see yourself and me in the water. You are no brother of the coyotes—you are my brother, for you look like me."

Bill looked in the spring and saw Chuck and himself in the water. He agreed. "We do look alike. Perhaps I am your brother!"

Chuck said, "Brother, you must put on some clothes and come with me to the ranch where I work and be a cowboy, too. But I don't have any extra clothes with me. I don't know what we can do!"

Pecos Bill laughed. "If anything has to be done, I can do it! Just a minute and I'll have some clothes!"

He looked around until he found a big old steer with horns measuring six feet from tip to tip. He grabbed it by the tail, yelled loudly, and scared it so badly that it jumped right out of its skin! (That didn't hurt the old steer. It wanted to grow a new hide anyhow.) From the hide Pecos Bill made himself a leather jacket, using a yucca thorn for a needle. He made some boots, too.

Then he made himself a pair of leather pants, the kind that are now called chaps. Other cowboys wear them now, to keep from getting scratched when riding through thorny bushes. They learned that from Pecos Bill.

When Bill had put on his clothes, Chuck told him, "Get up behind me on my cow pony, and he will carry both of us to the ranch."

But Pecos Bill laughed. "Ride your pony, and I'll go afoot, and I'll beat you to the ranch."

Sure enough, Bill galloped along easily, faster than Chuck's cow pony could run.

Chuck argued, though, "You really must not go up to the ranch on foot. Nobody walks in the ranch country. We must find you some old pony to ride, and a whip to urge him along with."

Just then Pecos Bill nearly stepped on the rattlesnake that lay in the trail. It was fifteen feet long and had thirty rattles on the end of its tail.

"Get out of my way," hissed Pecos in snake language.

"I won't," the snake hissed back. "I told Grampy long ago to teach you to stay out of my way."

The snake spit poison at Pecos Bill, hitting him right between the eyes. Bill said, "I'll give you three chances at me before I even begin to fight."

The three shots of poison didn't even blister Pecos Bill's skin. Next, Bill spit back at the snake, right on the top of the snake's head, and the snake fell over, unable to move for a moment.

Bill jumped on the snake and stamped it before

it had time to bite him. He caught the snake up by the throat and asked, "Had enough yet?"

The snake cried, "Yes, I give up!" Pecos Bill wrapped it around his arm and galloped on ahead of Chuck's pony.

Soon they met the mountain lion. He was the largest mountain lion in all the world, twice as large as Chuck's cow pony. The mountain lion growled, "I said I would eat you up if ever you got in my way, and now I will!"

He jumped at Pecos Bill, but Bill dodged and

pulled out a handful of the mountain lion's fur as he went by. The fight lasted for two hours. Every time the mountain lion tried to jump on Pecos Bill, Bill pulled out some more of his hair. The sky was so full of the mountain lion's hair that it was almost as dark as night.

Finally the lion lost all of his hair except just a little on the tips of his ears and under his chin. Then he begged, "Please, Pecos Bill, don't hurt me anymore."

"Very well," agreed Pecos Bill, "but you must let me ride you for a cow pony."

So Pecos Bill jumped on the mountain lion's back, and using the rattlesnake for a whip, rode on to the ranch with Chuck.

Just at sundown, Pecos Bill rode up to the cowboys' camp on the mountain lion, twice as big as a cow pony, and he was still using the rattlesnake fifteen feet long for a whip. The cowboys around the campfire were too surprised to say a word.

Chuck announced proudly, "Boys, this is my brother Pecos Bill."

Pecos Bill asked, "Who is the boss here?"

A big man seven feet tall and wearing three guns stepped forward. "I was," he said, "but you be now, Pecos Bill. Anybody that can ride a mountain lion and use a rattlesnake for a whip is boss here as long as he wants to be."

Pecos Bill soon tired of riding the mountain lion. It did not make a very good cow pony, because all the cattle were afraid of it. So Pecos Bill decided to get a real cow pony, and he asked the cowboys, "What's the very best horse in these parts?"

They answered, "The best horse in all the world is running loose in these very hills. He runs fast as the lightning, so we call him Lightning. Others call him the Pacing White Mustang, and some even say that his real name is Pegasus. We have all tried to catch him, but no one has ever got close enough to him to put a rope on him or even to see him clearly. We have chased him for days, riding our very best ponies and changing horses every two hours, but he outran all our best ponies put together."

But Pecos Bill told them, "I'll not ride a cow pony when I chase this horse. I can run faster than any of your ponies can."

So Pecos Bill threw his saddle and bridle over his shoulder and set out on foot to look for the famous wild white horse. When he got close enough to take a good look at Lightning, he saw that only the horse's mane and tail were a pure

white. The beautiful animal was really a light cream or pale gold color—the color of lightning itself.

Pecos Bill chased Lightning five days and four nights, all the way from Mexico across Texas and New Mexico and Arizona and Utah and Colorado and Wyoming and Montana, clear up to Canada, and then down to Mexico again. He had to throw away his saddle and bridle as they leaped across cactus-covered plains, down steep cliffs, and across canyons.

Finally Lightning got tired of running from Pecos Bill and stopped and snorted, "Very well,

I'll let you try to ride me if you think you can! Say your prayers and jump on!"

Pecos Bill smiled. "I say my prayers every night and every morning." And then he jumped on Lightning's back, gripping the horse's ribs with his knees and clutching the mane with his hands.

First, Lightning tried to run out from under Pecos Bill. He ran ten miles in twenty seconds! Next, he jumped a mile forward and two miles backward. Then he jumped so high in the air that Pecos Bill's head was up among the stars. Next, Lightning tried to push Pecos Bill off his back by running through clumps of mesquite trees. The thorns tore poor Bill's face and left his skin torn and bleeding.

When that failed, too, Lightning reared up on his hind legs and threw himself over backward. But Pecos Bill jumped off quickly, and before Lightning could get on his feet again, Bill sat down on his shoulders and held him firmly on the ground.

"Lightning," Pecos Bill explained, "you are the best horse in all the world, and I am the best cowboy in all the world. If you'll let me ride you, we will become famous together, and cowboys everywhere forever and forever will praise the deeds of Pecos Bill and Lightning." Then Pecos

Bill turned Lightning loose and said to him, "You may decide. You are free to go or to stay with me."

The beautiful horse put his nose in Pecos Bill's hand and said, "I want to stay with you and be your cow pony—the greatest cow pony in all the world."

Pecos Bill and Lightning went back and found the saddle and bridle where Bill had thrown them. Lightning let Pecos Bill put the saddle on him, but he didn't want to take the bit of the bridle into his mouth. So Pecos Bill just put a halter on him and guided him by pressure of the knees and by pulling on the reins of the halter.

Lightning would not let anybody but Pecos Bill ride him. Three-Gun Gibbs tried once, while Bill was not looking, but Lightning threw him so hard that he cracked the ground open where he fell. After that, the cowboys used to call Lightning Widow-maker.

SALLY ANN THUNDER ANN WHIRLWIND CROCKETT

RETOLD BY CARON LEE COHEN

Have you ever heard of Davy Crockett? He was an American hero who lived on the frontier in Tennessee. Davy wore a raccoon cap and carried a rifle that he called Betsy. Many stories tell about his great strength and his bravery.

In this tall tale, Davy Crockett has a wife named Sally Ann. She, too, is strong and brave. She fears nothing and is always ready to prove it!

SALLY Ann Thunder Ann Whirlwind Crockett lived long ago near the Mississippi River. Her husband was Davy Crockett. Now that lady was made of thunder with a little dash of whirlwind. She wore a beehive for a bonnet and a bearskin for a dress. Her toothpick was a bowie knife.

She could stomp a litter of wildcats and smash a band of starving wolves. She could outscream an eagle and outclaw a mountain lion.

She could skin a bear faster than an alligator swallows a fish.

She walked like an ox and ran like a fox.

She could wade the wide Mississippi without getting wet.

And she could jump over the Grand Canyon with both eyes shut.

She could do just about anything. And nothing on earth scared her. Nothing!

But she never bragged. And she never fought a man, woman, or critter for no good reason.

Now Mike Fink lived along the Mississippi, too. He was a bad man, always looking for a fight. He could beat any man except his enemy Davy Crockett. Their fights ended in a draw. And when Mike Fink wasn't fighting, he was bragging!

One day, Mike walked into a tavern. He jumped on a table and roared, "Half of me is wild horse and half is alligator. And the rest is crooked nails and red-hot snapping turtles. I can outrun, outshoot, outfight any man! If any man says that's not true, let him step up and fight."

No man dared to fight bad man Mike Fink. But Davy Crockett was in that tavern. And he was sick of hearing Mike Fink brag. "You don't scare me," Davy said. "And you couldn't even scare

my sweet little wife, Sally Ann Thunder Ann Whirlwind Crockett." Mike roared, "I'll bet you a dozen wildcats I can SCARE HER TEETH LOOSE!" And the bet was made.

So one evening, by the river, Mike found an alligator. He skinned it and crept inside the skin.

Then he crawled along the river. And there was Sally Ann Thunder Ann Whirlwind Crockett out for her nightly walk.

Mike crawled toward Sally Ann. He poked the alligator's head here and there. He opened its jaws big and wide. He let out a horrible cry.

He nearly scared himself out of the alligator's skin. But Sally Ann wasn't scared. Not one little bit. She just stepped aside as if that alligator were a dead stump.

So Mike crawled closer and stood up on his hind legs. Then he threw his front paws around Sally Ann.

Sally Ann Thunder Ann Whirlwind Crockett didn't let just any critter hug her. Her rage rose higher than a Mississippi flood.

Her eyes flashed lightning. The night sky lit up like day. Mike was scareder than a raccoon looking down a rifle barrel. But he thought of his bet with Davy Crockett. He kept circling Sally Ann and wagging his tail.

"That's enough, you worm!" said Sally Ann Thunder Ann Whirlwind Crockett. And she pulled out her toothpick.

With one swing, she cut off the head of that alligator. It flew fifty feet into the Mississippi River. Then she could see it was just bad man Mike Fink playing a trick.

"You lowly skunk!" she said. "Trying to scare a lady out on her nightly walk. Now stand up and fight like a man." She threw down her toothpick and rolled up her sleeves. She battered poor Mike till he fainted. She was still in a rage, but she wouldn't touch a man who was down. So she just walked off.

Mike didn't wake up till the next day. He couldn't tell his friends he had been beaten by a woman. Instead he bragged! "I got swallowed by an alligator. But I was chock full of fight and cut my way out. And here I am."

Still, a bet was a bet. So he caught a dozen wild-cats and gave them to Davy Crockett.

But that wasn't the end of it. One night down by the river, Sally Ann Thunder Ann Whirlwind Crockett met bad man Mike Fink.

Her rage rose higher than a Mississippi flood. She lit the sky with lightning from her eye.

And this time it scared Mike Fink's teeth loose.

From then on bad man Mike Fink had a mouth full of loose teeth. And every time he bragged, those teeth rattled!

JOHN DARLING

BY ANNE MALCOLMSON

Here's a tall tale of life in old New York State. It's about the famous Erie Canal and the people who steered the canal barges through its locks.

A man called John Darling really lived during the 1800s. But he never did all the things that happen in this tall tale. The real John Darling loved to boast and brag. Some say he's an even bigger liar than Paul Bunyan. Now you can see for yourself.

MANY, many stories have been told about the Erie Canal. One of them is the story of John Augustus Caesar Darling. John wasn't much as a little boy. He lived on a farm in upper New York State. He helped his father feed the pig and milk the cow. In the spring he went into the maple woods and helped hang the sugar buckets on their hooks. He pitched hay in the summer and gathered apples in the fall. That is about all we know about him then.

But as he grew older he became more interesting. He was about eleven years old when he first became important. His father sent him out to the field. He hitched the team of steers to the old wooden plow. As he moved up and down the furrow, he sang himself a song—a song that he loved dearly.

> "I've got a mule and her name is Sal,
> Fifteen miles on the Erie Canal.
> She's a good old worker and a good old pal,
> Fifteen miles on the Erie Canal."

As he sang to himself and to the steers, young John Augustus Caesar dreamed of the future. Some day he would own a boat. He would ride up and down the Erie Canal, like a king on his barge.

All of a sudden, John woke up from his dream.

He stopped singing. Right ahead of him loomed a big stump, at least six feet high. It was too late to turn away. Already the oxen had passed it, one on each side. Here were John and his plow, about to be stuck on the stump.

John Darling shut his eyes. He whipped his oxen and they pushed ahead. The old plow went right through the stump, with John after it. Yes, the stump split in two as clean as a whistle. John could hardly believe his eyes. He turned around to take another look at the stump. Just as he did so, the two halves rose up from the ground and fitted themselves together.

Now, things like that just don't happen to a plain ordinary farm boy. John Augustus Caesar Darling rubbed his eyes. He went back and felt the stump to make sure. There it was, as solid as a brick wall.

His family laughed at him when he told them what had happened. They didn't believe it at all. John himself, however, knew that he had had a sign. Some day he would be an important man. There was no doubt in his mind about that.

The following summer his remarkable powers were proved to his family. Mr. Darling, his father, noticed that the roof was leaking. He put the boys to work whittling shingles from pine boards. Then he propped a ladder against the side of the house. It was John's job to nail the shingles to the roof.

Unhappily, the weather was bad. A fog had rolled over the whole of upper New York State from Lake Ontario, as thick as pea soup. Even so, John put on his raincoat and climbed the ladder. He climbed to the very top and carried his shingles with him. One by one he fitted them in place and nailed them together.

All day long he worked. Shingle upon shingle, he hammered until the roof was finished. He had, in fact, made a whole new roof. He couldn't see it all at once to admire it because the fog was so thick.

When he climbed down again the sun came out and chased away the fog. Then John discovered his wonderful mistake. He had hammered the

shingles together twenty feet above the ridge-pole of the house. There hung his roof in mid-air. He had laid it on top of the fog.

As a grown man, John Darling first went to work as a "sugarbush" man. In other words, he had a stand of maple-sugar trees. He loved to go out into the woods and tap the trees when the sap began to run. Into each he inserted a short pipe, and under each pipe he hung a bucket. Then, when the sap had collected in the buckets, he took them home. He boiled and boiled until his kettles were sticky with delicious maple syrup. He was particularly fond of maple syrup on buckwheat cakes. All winter long he had his favorite dish for breakfast.

The thing that finally discouraged him from the maple-sugar business was the mosquito. As you know, mosquitoes love sweets. They used to hover around Darling's maple trees. They were as large as airplanes. Their buzz-buzz-buzz sounded as loud as the hum of a sawmill. They stung the farm hands when they came to collect the sap. They stung even John himself.

At last John thought of a way to be rid of them. His sap pans were large iron kettles. Into one of these he put some pure maple sugar. Then he turned it upside down under one of his trees. He hid himself inside, his big hammer in his hand. Sure enough! The mosquitoes smelled it. They came from miles around to nibble at the sugar. But the iron kettle was in their way. Buzz-buzz-buzz! They put their stingers to work. They bored through the iron kettle until they reached the soft sweet sugar beneath it.

John was too smart for them. As each stinger bored through the iron, John came up with his hammer. He flattened the mosquito's bill against the inside of the kettle.

Within an hour all the mosquitoes were safely fastened to the sap pan. They were so angry they buzzed like a hangar full of planes.

But there was nothing they could do about it. At last they lifted their wings and off they flew. They took John Darling's sap pan with them, firmly fixed to their bills.

Before long, John Augustus Caesar Darling tired of farming. The "Erie Canal" song ran through his head until it nearly drove him mad.

> "Low bridge, everybody down!
> Low bridge, for we're going through a town,
> And you'll always know your neighbor,
> You'll always know your pal,
> If you ever navigated on the Erie Canal."

You can see for yourself how John must have felt. As he followed the plow he couldn't help singing, "Low bridge." Even the steers thought he was a little silly. There wasn't a bridge anywhere near the cornfield.

At last he couldn't stand it any longer. He sold his farm and his sugar trees and went to Albany. There he bought himself a canal boat, a beautiful boat. He painted it white and named it the *Erie Queen*. He fitted up the captain's cabin with his favorite possessions. This was a home after his own heart.

John filled up the hold of the *Erie Queen* with shoes and watches and plows and started off for Buffalo. John's old horse plodded along the towpath, pulling the boat. Sometimes John walked beside the horse, smoking his pipe. Sometimes he sat on deck in the sun, his big face shining with pleasure.

It was perfectly all right for him to sing the Canal song now. After all, you don't feel silly bawling out, "Low bridge, everybody down," when there is a low bridge ahead of you.

Up and down the Canal slid the *Erie Queen*. When she reached Buffalo, John unloaded his watches and shoes and plows. He sold them to the pioneers who were moving west into Ohio and Indiana. Sometimes he sold them to the captains of the Great Lakes ships. They took them even farther west, up through the Great Lakes to Wisconsin and Minnesota to the Swedes and Norwegians.

When John had sold his wares, he bought others.

From the Lake captains and Western farmers he bought lumber and coal and hay. Then he and the *Erie Queen* headed back to Buffalo. Here he sold his cargo to the Eastern merchants.

Back and forth, back and forth, from Albany to Buffalo, back and forth moved John Darling, as happy as a king.

To cook his meals John Darling hired a young woman named Sal. He claimed that she was the original "Sal" of the song, "the very best cook on the Erie Canal." She made buckwheat cakes that were as light as goose down.

She was more than a good cook, however. She was a remarkable woman. Sal was over six feet tall, freckled, cross-eyed, and twenty-three years old. She was indeed a daisy. Furthermore, she had red hair, so red it outshone the glory of the sunsets. It glowed like a whole cluster of fireflies. In fact, on dark nights, John had Sal sit in the bow of the boat. He used her for a headlight.

Before long, John Darling was completely in love. The only thing he needed to make his happiness perfect was Sal. Sal, however, had many other beaux. Every boatman, every lock-keeper was in love with her, too. Whenever John asked her to marry him, she said, "No!"

At last he persuaded her to give him a chance.

She arranged to hold a contest. All the Canalmen were great fishermen. On quiet afternoons they liked to trail their fishing lines over the sides of their boats. Often they caught enough pickerel or perch for their suppers. Sal agreed that she would marry the man who caught the most fish on one certain day.

All her other suitors, of course, were told about the contest. They fixed up their fishing tackle. They brushed their beards and combed their mustaches, and put on their best store clothes. On the proper day they came together at the meeting place.

The contest began at midnight and lasted until the following midnight. Twenty-four hours in which to catch a bride!

John Augustus Caesar Darling, handsome in his new suit, sat at the bow of the *Erie Queen*. Up and down the Canal, as far as one could see, were the boats of his rivals. Each of the men held a fishing line in his hand.

Unfortunately, the other suitors had good luck. They reeled in their lines, one after another, until their decks were piled with fish. Poor old John had not a nibble. He jiggled his fishing pole, but nothing happened. He sat perfectly still. Nothing happened. By noon he had not a fish to his name.

By sundown the other suitors were growing tired. They had been hauling in bass and perch all day long, and were ready to quit. Most of them gave up and started to count their catch. But not John. He sat on the deck of the *Erie Queen*, sadly holding his fishing pole. His big tank was still empty. Not a fish.

Meanwhile, Sal had been watching the contest from the bank. She saw John and his empty tank. She felt sorry for him, because she really wanted him to win.

As soon as it was dark she climbed aboard his barge. John was surprised to see her. Her beautiful red hair shone like the tail of a comet. It lit up the whole Canal.

This gave John an idea. "Put your head over the side," he said softly to Sal. She did as he told her. The light from her hair gleamed out across the black water to the other bank. In its path swam a school of fat black bass.

The fish were attracted by the light. They acted like moths around the flame of a candle. One by one they jumped into John's boat. They didn't wait for him to catch them on his line.

"Now put your head over the other side," John whispered to Sal. He was afraid to startle the fish. There, in the path of the light, swam a school of pickerel. One by one they, too, jumped out of the water onto the deck of the *Erie Queen*. They didn't even wait to be invited.

With Sal's help, John Darling soon had his hold full of squirming, fine fish. The decks also were piled high with them. When at last the village clock sounded midnight, he and Sal were knee deep in perch and bass and bullheads.

The judging took place in the courthouse. The other Canalmen swaggered in with their catches. Each was sure that he had won Sal's hand. Imagine the dismay when John came in. The judges counted his fish. Without any question at all, they had to admit that he had won the contest. Sal tried to look surprised when John claimed her. But everyone could see that she was more pleased than surprised.

They were soon married. John Darling took his bride to Niagara Falls for their honeymoon. When they returned to the *Erie Queen*, the neighbors gathered and gave them a big party. They had songs and dancing and a fish fry and maple syrup and buckwheat cakes. It was a great success.

From then on, John's happiness was complete. He used to sing out his favorite song at the top of his lungs. People two miles away could tell he was coming when they heard him shout, "Low bridge, everybody down."

He changed the verse a little, though. Instead of singing, "I've got a mule, and her name is Sal," he sang,

> "I've got a wife, and her name is Sal,
> Fifteen miles on the Erie Canal.
> She's a good old worker and a good old pal,
> The very best cook on the Erie Canal."

Acknowledgments

Grateful acknowledgment is made to the following authors and publishers for the use of copyrighted materials. Every effort has been made to obtain permission to use previously published material. Any errors or omissions are unintentional.

The Caxton Printers for "The Winter of the Blue Snow" from *Paul Bunyan Swings His Axe* by Dell J. McCormick. Copyright © 1936 by Dell J. McCormick.

Delacorte Press, a division of Bantam, Doubleday, Dell Publishing Group, Inc. for "Oonagh and the Giants" from *The Skull in the Snow and Other Folktales* by Toni McCarty. Copyright © 1981 by Toni McCarty.

Doubleday, a division of Bantam, Doubleday, Dell Publishing Group, Inc. for "The Tall Tales" by I. K. Junne from *Floating Clouds, Floating Dreams* by I. K. Junne. Copyright © 1974 by I. K. Junne.

Roberta Strauss Feuerlicht for Chapters 1 and 2 (Retitled: "Young Paul Bunyan") from *The Legends of Paul Bunyan* by Roberta Strauss Feuerlicht. Copyright © 1966.

Greenwillow Books, a division of William Morrow and Co., Inc. for *Sally Ann Thunder Ann Whirlwind Crockett* retold by Caron Lee Cohen, illustrated by Ariane Dewey. Text copyright © 1985 by Caron Lee Cohen. Illustrations copyright © 1985 by Ariane Dewey.

Houghton Mifflin Company for "Pecos Bill" from *Pecos Bill and Lightning* by Leigh Peck. Copyright © 1940 by Leigh Peck. Copyright © renewed 1968 by Leigh Peck; "John Darling" from *Yankee Doodle's Cousins* by Anne Malcolmson. Copyright © 1941 by Anne Burnett Malcolmson. Copyright © renewed 1969 by Anne Malcolmson von Storch.

Julian Messner, a division of Simon & Schuster, Inc. for "Once There Was and Once There Was Not" from *Tales the People Tell in Russia* by Lee Wyndham. Copyright © 1970 by Lee Wyndham.

Illustrations

Ed Parker: pp. 6-15; Arieh Zeldich: pp. 16-21; D. J. Simison: pp. 22-29; Lyle Miller: cover, pp. 30-43; Arvis Stewart: pp. 44-57; Ariane Dewey: pp. 58-65; Rosekrans Hoffman: pp. 66-79.